DRAGTASTIC

The legendary book of fun, facts and fabulosity

Foreword by
Panti Bliss

Written by
Crystal Rasmussen OBE

Illustrated by
Richard Williams

BLOOMSBURY CARAVEL

LONDON · OXFORD · NEW YORK · NEW DELHI · SYDNEY

BLOOMSBURY CARAVEL
Bloomsbury Publishing Plc
50 Bedford Square, London, WC1B 3DP, UK

BLOOMSBURY, BLOOMSBURY CARAVEL and the Diana logo are trademarks of
Bloomsbury Publishing Plc

First published in Great Britain 2019

A catalogue record for this book is available from the British Library

Library of Congress Cataloguing-in-Publication data has been applied for

ISBN: PB: 978-1-4482-1699-4

2 4 6 8 10 9 7 5 3 1

Designed by Plum5 Ltd

Printed in China by RRD Asia Printing Solutions Limited

Bloomsbury Publishing Plc makes every effort to ensure that the papers used in the manufacture
of our books are natural, recyclable products made from wood grown in well-managed forests.
Our manufacturing processes conform to the environmental regulations of the country of origin

To find out more about our authors and books visit
www.bloomsbury.com and sign up for our newsletters

Contents

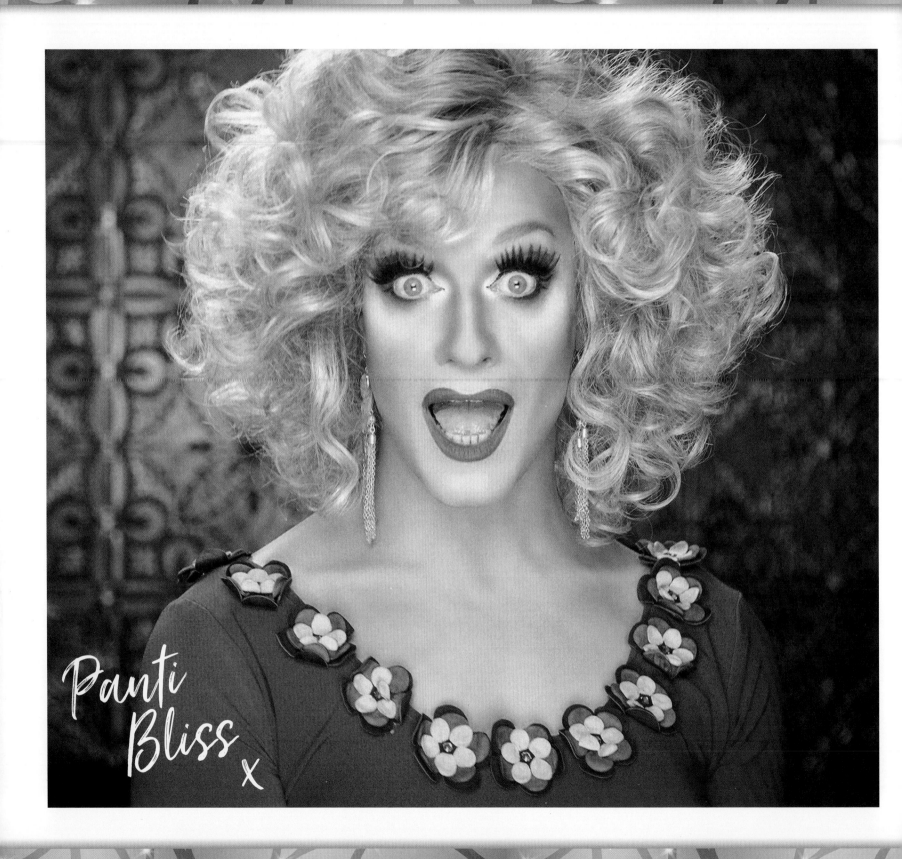

Panti
Bliss x

Foreword

Drag is more popular than ever right now – it's having a cultural *moment*. You can't swing a lace-front wig within two hundred yards of a gay bar these days without taking out a couple of baby drags. And good for them.

Because drag is fun! It's inherently punk, an act of defiance, a two fingers to social expectations – and that's always exciting! It's a kind of superpower.

Drag queens were often the kids who spent their school years not drawing attention to themselves. They learnt the fine art of invisibility as a defence mechanism – because it was safer to go unnoticed.

And then one day they see their first drag queen. And she's not invisible. She's not blending into the background. She's covered in sequins to make damn sure she doesn't! She's *demanding* attention. She's *anti*-invisible!

She's not terrified a limp wrist will betray her. Not trying to suppress any hint of terrifying femininity. Hell no! She has taken all the things they tried to sneer out of her, and is throwing them back as *strengths*. As *fun*!

She is giving all the assholes the glittered finger and it's the most beautiful thing ever.

And you want a piece of that, right? Course you do Gurl! But you're confused. Course you are Miss Thing. Where to even start?! Well calm your nerves, because Crystal Rasmussen and Richard Williams have put together this fun guide to get you started. Let them lead you gently through a brief history of man-sized feet squeezed into lady-sized shoes, with a handy glossary of vocabulary so you won't embarrass yourself by not knowing your *tea* from your *shade*. Then let them introduce you to a line-up of classic queens to help inspire you. They'll even help you find the perfect name for the new, more fabulous you.

In fact, calling this a mere "book" does it a disservice! It's *much* more than that.

It's a passport to a whole new you.

Introduction

Why is there such a fuss about drag?

Is it the colours? Or the sequins? The wigs? The makeup?

Of course, the sensory elements of drag are absolutely something to make a fuss about. Stepping into a sumptuous dress, and out of your boring gender, is the most stunning way to spend a Saturday night — trust me! But drag isn't simply the buying and wearing of these fabulous, subversive, glittering markers. It's not about what these markers are, it's about what donning them means.

Through choosing to vacate the world the way it's been given to you, drag forces you to question it. It asks you to step, stiletto first, into a world of radical history, broken-down gender systems, and sumptuously savage wit. Drag represents a world where anything is possible: a world where someone can take such hotly gendered codes and signifiers and put them together to transgress strict binaries, to create a whole new person and, if lucky, a whole new family of their own. Drag allows you to be anything you want to be.

That's why people who come to drag often devote their lives to it. To a precarious pay cheque and a rota of late nights; to pricey costumes; to damaged skin and cracked nail beds; to bouts of scary homophobia and blistered feet. Because, beyond all that, drag allows you to become the kind of superstar you never thought you'd be allowed to be. Go to any drag show on a Saturday night and you'll see countless queens and kings giving Mariah Carey and Zayn Malik a run for their money. Drag is radical. Drag allows you a place to break those rules in the rulebook again and again.

Drag gives you a new perspective, allowing you to pull back the curtain and glimpse a glittering world where you're free of restrictions. It's a healing aid, a therapy, and it's so beautiful in all of its forms.

Think of this book as your starter pack: inside it you'll find a bunch of queens with varied and distinct characters, ones which will hopefully give you a sense of how far this community of superstars really spans.

There's a drag queen dictionary, because learning the language is fundamental. There are quizzes, design challenges and a chance for you to find out what kind of drag really suits you.

And while drag is probably the most fun you can have with your clothes on, the fuss is about more than just fun. It's about love — for yourself, for your sisters and brothers and mamas and papas. It's about giving back to people, and saving a bit for yourself. It's about being the most glorious person in the room, while pulling everyone up to your level. It's about proving that, while you might be an outcast, you're quicker, cooler and funnier than the people on the inside. It's about proving that being a misfit makes you the best person of all.

So go forth and educate yourselves. Remember: this book is a wonderful guide, but there's no way paper pages can translate the unadulterated ecstasy you might find on the streets, in the clubs and pubs and theatres around the world. So, when you're ready, take your new persona off the page and into the streets: that's where the real magic happens.

History

To understand drag, one must first understand its history, its herstory.

More than anything else, our role as drag performers is to uphold a glorious tradition: a tradition of resistance and response, as well as a respect for those who came before us. We honour our forebears — those who provided us not only with techniques for painting a face or cinching a waist, but with a bank of incisive references, a beautiful, expressive lexicon, a glowing depiction of the power of family, and a political vigour which won us a newfangled respect and a bunch of integral rights. We owe our freedom to be drag performers to the most radical of our predecessors, and by keeping their legacies alive we are contributing to that same energy which created such beauty and such change.

Being a drag performer isn't solely about one's individual elegance, face and grace: it's about creating a world where you can run free, and live out your wildest childhood fantasies.

A drag performer is a kind of cultural shaman-cum-diva: our costume and our persona give us a free pass to comment on and critique the things society needs to look at, from a broken system to bad sex, and everything in between, queen!

Drag, for many who engage in it, is like a religion. A religion which replaces God with makeup and the Holy Scripture with a huge pop-cultural back-catalogue. It's a lifestyle full of codes and values which we uphold as we slick dried-up liner onto our eyes and irremovable glue to the lace on our foreheads. But before the drag we know now existed — the one tethered to flamingly queer sexualities and genders and cultures that stray from the normal — drag was merely the act of dressing in the wares of another gender, for other kinds of religious purposes.

From Ancient Egypt to the Aztecs, Grecian theatre to Incan ceremony: cross-dressing was used across cultures to invoke the powers of certain gods during religious ceremonies and rituals. A different type of religious use, entirely, but still pretty diva.

In Japan, the tradition of another type of drag finds its groundings in Kabuki and Noh theatre, the latter of which rose to popularity in the 14th century, the former in the 17th. Both types of traditional theatre found their basis in specific types of ceremonial practices. In Noh dance, actors wearing masks would follow set routines in a dance associated with rice planting and fertility, while in Kabuki — the much more widely known and less ritualistic of the two practices — female impersonators would be carefully made up, speak in moderated voices and move in ways that evoked the essence of femaleness, of femininity.

Around the same time in Britain, drag performance became an important tool in religious theatre: with women excluded from any religious practice, men would dress in female garb to depict female characters in theatrical retellings of Bible stories. Eventually, these performances became less directly linked to the church, and as made-up subplots were added to these once religious demonstrations, modern theatrics was born.

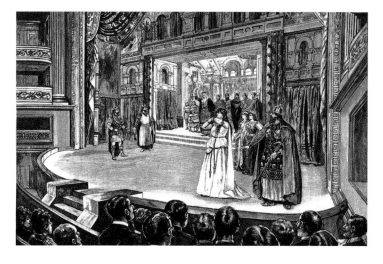

This was the same throughout Shakespeare's era, when lithe young boys would be offered the female parts — in fact many believe Shakespeare can be credited with the invention of the term "drag" — meaning Dressed As A Girl, as written in the stage directions of his comedy *As You Like It*. Castratos would play women in opera, the dame in a pantomime would be played by a working class bloke, and drag — while still, at this point, totally unlinked to homosexuality — was in common use, across cultures, for entertainment purposes. And it still excluded women.

Until the late 19th century, that is, when women and men began to develop acts in Cabaret clubs and Vaudeville theatres. Acts which played with gendered stereotypes for entertainment and comedic purposes — a glorious middle finger to the system.

It wasn't until the 1930s that drag began to look like what we know it as today: a lifeline for the queer community, a pure distillation of our camp culture, a glittering, glorious world away from the boredom of prohibition and, swiftly, war. The relatively new scientific field of sexology had defined a "third gender" — as an effeminate man or a masculine woman — and by the mid '30s it was popular knowledge that those who donned drag of any sort were most probably of this third gender. These performers would be found at private parties, until the early gay bars emerged in the fifties. This was the tipping point, the reclamation of drag culture from straight men in theatre to the queers of the bars and clubs that emerged alongside gay culture. We've been here from the beginning, working every room. And, naturally, heterosexuality began to distance itself from the forms of cross-dressing it had explored for centuries: eager to shed associations with an increasingly criminalised queer community.

Through the '50s and '60s, drag separated into female impersonation — members of the famous Revue shows which toured the States and performed their flawless female impersonation for mostly heterosexual audiences would be outraged at being likened to drag queens or kings, who were of the lower-classes, the gay bars and the streets (the best places!).

But the modern, much celebrated, incarnation of drag was born out of these bars and clubs, and while it became increasingly celebrated here — with queens and kings venerated as icons of their scenes in the underground worlds of the illegal gay bars — female impersonation was mocked in the public eye in movies.

We resided in clubs, and bars, with blacked out windows or no windows at all. Until, in June 1969, the Stonewall riots broke out, with the first brick of resistance thought to have been cast by trans woman of colour and drag performer Marsha P. Johnson. "Somebody that puts on a pink t-shirt one day a year then goes back to their office job, that wasn't who started Stonewall. It was people like us, who were out on the street, doing drag, and we'd had enough!" the legendary New York institution

Lady Bunny would say later in an interview. And from the silently political, to the heart of the public eye; it was here that the Gay Liberation Movement began, a series of fights and years of resistance which would sow the seeds for the undoing of much homophobic and transphobic legislation which worked against us at the time.

Through the 1980s, drag became more popular in the mainstream — drag was still sequestered to the underground, but that underground became riotously in demand, the coolest place to be, of course! New York's East Village performance scene proffered iconic and important nights like Wigstock, founded by Lady Bunny, and The Pyramid, on which she was a fixture; Divine rose to fame as a grotesque movie star who ate dog shit at the end of *Pink Flamingos*; and *Paris is Burning*, the 1990 documentary, captured the Harlem Vogueing scene of '80s New York, and would go on to inform, be celebrated and then appropriated by much popular culture of the time.

Through the '90s, club kids like Michael Alig, Amanda LePore, and Leigh Bowery offered cross-continental new modes of drag and gender performance, and these gender fuckers became the most fashionable guests on talk shows and runways, and were the absolute

definition of the party. Around the same time, in the mid '90s, *Priscilla Queen of the Desert*, *To Wong Foo, Thanks for Everything! Julie Newmar*, and *Wigstock the Movie* offered new, mainstream ways for people to access drag and queer performance and lives in a completely new context, where we weren't the butt of the joke, but were brilliant artists full of love and an alternative way of seeing.

And no history of drag would be complete without RuPaul, who made it big in her various music video appearances, most notably Love Shack by the B-52s. From here, she steadily climbed, in heels and a gorgeously ratty wig, to her current status as the most famous drag queen in the world. And, in 2009, Mama Ru brought her platform to a global stage with the birth of RuPaul's *Drag Race*: arguably responsible for the mainstreaming of conversations about drag, queerness and the beauty so much of this scene holds.

While the show has its valid critiques — often showing a limited conception of drag, and only recently allowing an openly trans contestant for example — it has played a huge part in bringing us to where we are today.

But, truly, as was always the case in drag: the most exciting, radical, boundary breaking drag performers exist in the bars, the clubs,

the niche theatres and the spaces which are very much needed by queer people in order to survive. From one religion to another, drag is one of the most important parts of queer culture, a culture and an art form which has saved countless lives for countless decades.

But drag's history isn't over: while there are fights to fight, dominant cultures to resist, and raucous amounts of fun to be had, drag will continue to provide a space for people to undermine overbearing normality; it will continue to allow people to push back against intolerance and violence; it will arm us with the tools to fight for acceptance exactly on our terms, not wrapped in the perfectly acceptable package society would wish upon us.

Drag is both the definition and reflection of queer culture. No single written history could do justice to the colours, the energy, the power and all the people who have built such a rich, limitless culture. A culture which continues to give so many, who would have otherwise been deprived, the opportunity to be free, to dream. The world is brimming with superstars in the shape of drag performers who, for a good tip, will show you what real superstardom looks like. So go out and support your local diva!

Dress your Queens

Now, to build your look: it's the first thing your adoring audience will see when they behold your beauty. It's not the most important thing about your drag, but it's an important place to start. Whether you're a fashion queen, a messy diva or a butch king, constructing the look is all about reference, character and who you want to be. Dive into the stickers, you can find them in the middle of the book: where there are outfits, wigs and shoes ready to construct an iconic look with.

Kimono Cobain

Kimono, or Kim to her sisters, is known for her lip-sync skills. Usually a quiet creature, the moment her stilletos hit the stage she has full command of the crowd. Gracious and intelligent, Kimono combines the new and old schools of drag: big looks and bigger wigs, with a fierce commitment to the history of drag culture and a welcoming attitude to newer, greener queens. She's been beating her face in her parents' bathroom since she was fourteen, and moved to San Francisco the moment she could afford the bus ticket. Here, in the Castro, she fell in with The House of Cobain and quickly rose up the scene. Her favourite drink is the blood of her enemies, and she loves vintage European movies, ostrich feathers and the work of Audre Lorde.

Sheola L'amour

While *l'amour* is the only word she knows in French, Sheola is all about the chic and is *never* seen without the perfect accessories, a cinched waist, and shoes which never match her clutch. "That's just tacky!" Known for her dancing, legend has it that Sheola once did the jump splits from the top of a double decker bus during a gay party brunch in Fort Lauderdale.

She loves the beach and despises Donald Trump. Her favourite food is sushi — until she's drunk, when she often eats a tub of peanut butter with her fingers. She is known for the catch phrase "Sheola will show ya!" which she's actually very bored of saying. She's working on her first album, "The Sheola Show," which is music she wants people to vogue to.

Glangela Fever

Glangela is one of London's most iconic queens. She's been on and off the drag scene since the '90s, and has a penchant for disappearing with a lover or three for weeks, months, and one time a year, to Berlin. But every time she comes back you can count on the fact she'll have stocked her armoury with more drag tools than you can shake an eyelash at: reinventing herself each time, a phoenix from glittering ashes. Unlike most queens, Glangela doesn't enjoy lip-syncing, and chooses instead to sing live. From classics like Whitney's *I Will Always Love You* and Rage Against the Machine's *Killing in the Name*, to her original pop-punk tracks, Glangela is adored for her creativity. You can catch her at Bethnal Green Working Men's Club playing the synth with acrylic nails.

Bertie Brecht

Bertie is a theatre queen who spends most of her days writing awful musicals and putting them on in niche theatres across San Diego. It doesn't matter that they're terrible though, because she's the funniest queen on the scene, who can make even the most dire sketches sidesplittingly funny. Her drag is one based around politics — using her humour to critique normative structures and a shambolic Trump administration. Her favourite TV show is *Desperate Housewives*, because every episode is named after a Stephen Sondheim song, and she bases most of her character on Bree Van de Kamp, but with more outrageous clothes. Before she was a drag queen full time, she was in training to become a lawyer. Her dream is to play the first ever drag queen on a mainstream telenovela.

Florentina

She's a baby queen on the Houston scene but Florentina has already made a huge splash. She's just turned eighteen, but has spent the last four years working on her makeup, every night, in her bedroom. She can sew, she can style, she can lay wigs, and she is already taking sewing commissions from other queens across Texas who obsess over her flawlessness on social media. Although she's making waves on the net, ingratiating herself onto the club scene has come with its bumps — some of the more established queens are clearly intimidated by Flo's perfection. With a little time, and a little humility, she'll be a stalwart on the scene before she knows it; intimidation of the younger queens is a rite of passage. Her favourite fabric is crushed velvet, and her favourite time of the week is Sunday Mass, especially after she's spent a night at Church — the best drag club in town.

Jennifer Ho-Pez

J-Ho is hilarious. A New York queen, originally hailing from McComb in Mississippi, she's a spokesperson for chunky queens everywhere. Her schtick is that she was in the same year at school as Britney Spears: "I could've been a global superstar, I'm from a trailer park too!" Obsessed with old Hollywood, her polished looks and her filthy persona are hilariously at odds. Jennifer makes money, mainly, by hosting gay weddings and hysterical hen parties. While she's an avid watcher of RuPaul's *Drag Race*, she's never applied because she thinks she'd have to sanitise her outrageous humour she's spent so many years perfecting. Her least favourite Hollywood star is Mae West because she believes she could've been her had she been born decades earlier. Her favourite dance move is the Take a Seat and Make Them Applaud.

Constantine Commotion

As one of Perth's premier entertainers, Constantine is truly overflowing with savage reads. People go to her shows desperate for a front row seat, just to be picked on by the queen of the takedown. Nobody's safe. But, really, Ms. Commotion is all about community: donating her entire tip bucket to a different LGBTQ charity each week. She's also known for having the biggest clan of drag daughters in Perth. She used to work in an office, as a paralegal, but when her drag show started to gain notoriety she ditched the suit and tie for a full time wig and heels. "The only thing I miss is staring at the repressed lawyers in their tight shirts." While she loves to keep fit, she prefers ice cream and beer.

Gina Gee-Wizz

Gina has been a jobbing queen for nearly two decades — born of the European club scene of the '90s, she still finds all her looks on budget rave-wear online stores or in Camden's iconic Cyber Dog. Gina transitioned in the mid-2000s, and has since been running a cabaret night for trans queens and kings in an arts club in West London. Her commitment to empowering trans voices in the drag community has made her somewhat of a legend on the scene, a mother still for many young trans and gender non-conforming kings and queens. Drag is her full-time job, and while at points money has been really tight, she has never once wavered in her commitment to her art and her politics. Her favourite colour is feathers, and her favourite movie is *Top Gun*.

Kum-Kwat

Kum-Kwat is a powerful queen, an unstoppable force on the Sydney scene. She's a female drag queen, but resists the need to be categorised by that, and has starred in countless documentaries and short films about what it means to explore femininity. But that's not all she explores — her drag focusses on the intersection of race and gender, her style is iconically Afrofuturist, and her performances centre on sci-fi and space and escaping the plane on which we all exist, for dimensions more radical. She runs a witches' coven from her basement. Her favourite food is cheese — every kind of cheese — except goat's cheese, which she can't stand.

Donna Summers

Donna Summers is a muscle queen who's incredibly proud of her body. She avoids padding, and enjoys flexing her toned physique on stage. While some of her detractors think she might be too obsessed with her masculine body, she works hard to uplift queens of all body types. In one particularly renowned performance, she bench pressed her best friend — a chunky queen known simply as Mamma. Known to her Vegas sisters as an outrageous queen who earns the most tips, she certainly doesn't want to be known for relying on her body. She claims her favourite food is a protein shake, but actually it's lemon meringue pie!

The Huntress

The Huntress is a dancer who works the poles at Metropolis every weekend. She rose up through the London scene quickly — starting out by dragging up with friends and going to every queer night on the circuit. Spotted by an older queen on the scene, The Huntress — or Hunty for short — was quickly drafted into the House of Savage in which she became an incredibly active member: as the resident choreographer, teaching the queens routines for their weekly shows at Her Upstairs. She lives in Essex, which is where she gets her adoration for anything sparkling. By day The Huntress is a hairdresser who is known for her incredible gift for making even the smallest of hair absolutely massive. Her signature look is wearing a giant tail which matches her wig: "A unicorn among queens!"

Lactasia

One yelp review of Lactasia's weekly Brooklyn show calls it "utterly baffling, but in the best way". It's on a Monday, and she invites young queens to come down to give a guest showing each week. Whether it's joke contemporary dance recitals or pretending to eat fake babies, it's "radical art" which often doesn't make much sense, but when it's great it's incredible. Lactasia's countenance is sickly-sweet-cum-murderous — like a Stepford Wife on acid. Her favourite musical is *Starlight Express*, and her favourite word is "bleach". When she's not in drag, she works in the city as a banker — two worlds which she keeps distinctly separate. She's always got the best costumes and the best wigs, which is why she doesn't quit the banking world: "Radical art doesn't really pay the rent."

Colour your Queens

Colour can signify so many things; emotions, moods, unspoken histories. In the hanky code of the '70s, gay men could indicate their fancies without speaking a word. Looking for a top? Keep your eyes open for a navy bandanna worn on the right. Of course drag queens can get away with anything so don't worry about the "rules", throw the book away and do your own thing. After all, rules are made to be broken.

'We're all born *naked* and the rest *is drag!*'

RUPAUL

When a gay man has *way too much fashion sense* for one gender, he is a *drag queen!*

NOXEEMA JACKSON

'When in doubt, freak 'em out!'

SHARON NEEDLES

'If I hadn't been a woman, I'd be a drag queen for sure'

DOLLY PARTON

It doesn't matter what you look like! I mean if you have a hunchback, just throw *a little glitter* on it, honey, and go **dancing!**

JAMES ST. JAMES

Design your Drag

Drag artists embody so many kinds of style: whether a scream queen in a horror movie realness or a teenage king in a perfectly messy high school uniform, the key to the perfect drag outfit isn't just colour, sparkles and cinching. While all of these things are absolutely integral to the making of a glorious, memorable look, the heart of any successful outfit is imagination. Whether it's the perfect blend of brilliantly camp references, or a brand new silhouette nobody's ever seen before, drag is supposed to take what we know and flip the table. So, grab your stickers and flip the table!

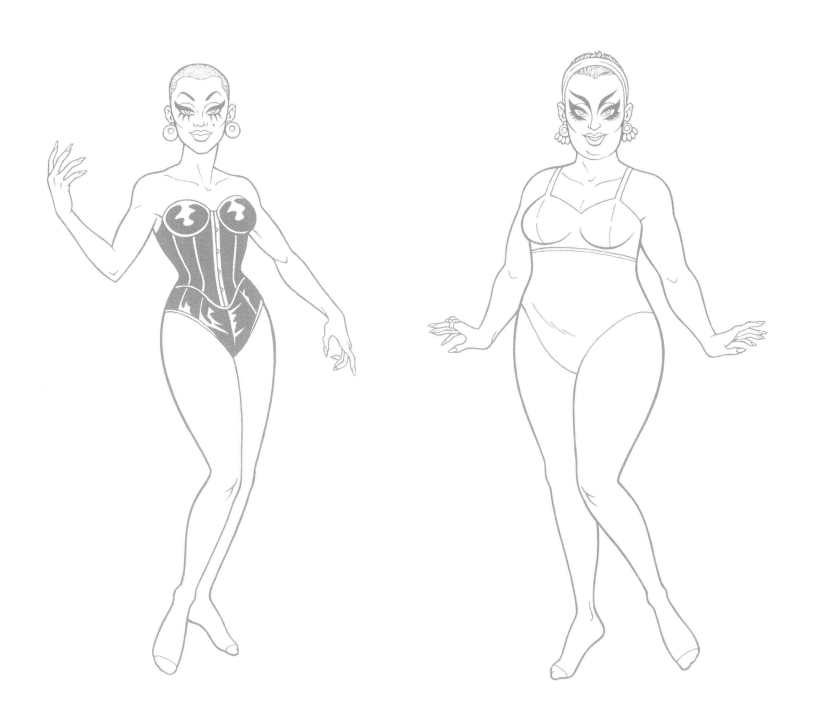

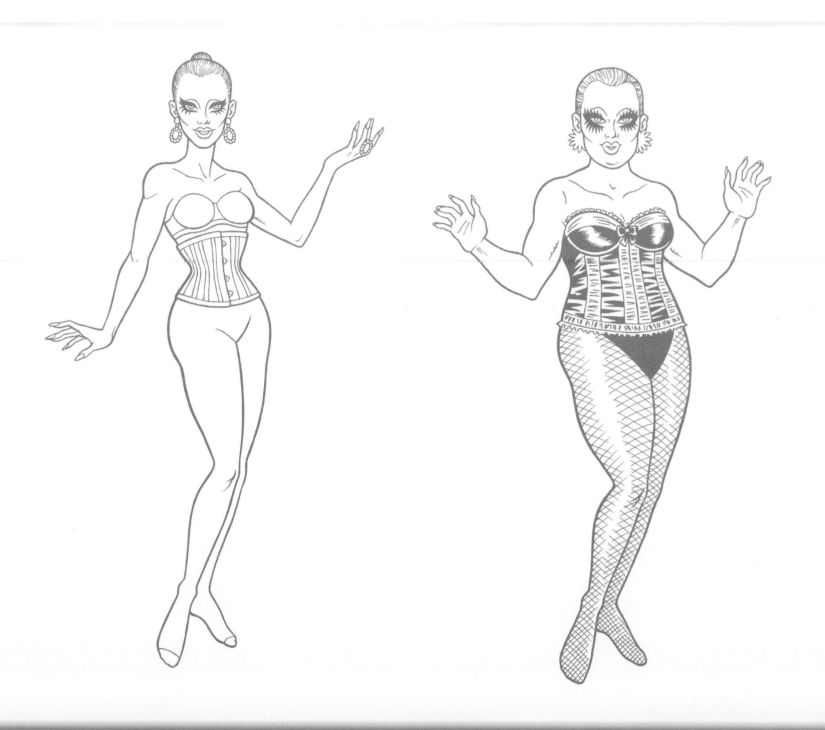

Drag Queen Dictionary

Queer people have communicated in secret linguistic codes FOREVER — whether with the hidden language of Polari or the beautifully descriptive words born out of the New York vogueing scene, queer people have been using concealed, expressive words to describe the way they live, on their terms, for decades. Drag continues this tradition — with ingenious colloquialisms that link up people across scenes and across the world. Below is a dictionary of some of these words, but before you use them try to ensure where their origins lie: some words simply aren't some people's to use. Some words, however, are.

BAR QUEEN (n) — An insult, used to describe a drag queen who only performs in small bars. "Honey, she's only a bar queen."

BEAT (v) — the motion of constantly dabbing a makeup sponge or brush against the face, to create a flawless look. "Gurl, she beat!"

BIND (n) — when a person bandages down their breasts to give them the appearance of a flat chest. "My bind is so tight!"

BODY-ODY-ODY (n) — A more exciting word for body. "Damn, she's serving body-ody-ody!"

BOOBIE BIB (n) — A breast plate, made of silicone or rubber, to give a queen the appearance of real breasts. Titty bib also acceptable.

BOOGER (n) — A queen who looks busted or messy. An insult often thrown at a queen or king who's bad at makeup/hair/dressing themselves. "She's a true booger."

BREEDER (n) — An insult used to describe a heterosexual, or sex which has the potential for procreation. "Gurl, there were so many breeders in the house tonight!"

BUTCH QUEEN (n) — A masculine-looking drag queen.

COOKING/BAKING (v) — To apply foundation, concealer or powder to your face, allowing it to reach body temperature to make it more blendable. "I'm just cooking!"

CHICKEN CUTLETS (n) — A colloquialism for the pads a queen or king uses to give them the shape of the desired gender they're performing.

CLOCK (v) — To spot what someone is trying to hide / to point out a person's flaws. "Clock the mug!"

DEATH DROP (n) — A dance move originating from vogueing: a drop to the floor, with one leg extended, one leg bent beneath you. "Did you see that death drop? Right on the beat!"

DRAG KING (n) — A person who uses costume and signifiers to perform and explore masculinity. "He's the best drag king in town."

DRAG MOTHER (n) — An older or more experienced drag queen. She often acts as a mentor or teacher to a younger, up-and-coming drag queen. "Don't you dare come for my Drag mom!"

DRAG FAMILY (n) — A collection of drag queens or kings, who take on the same surname and resources. "I'm part of the Family Fierce!"

DRAG SISTER (n) — The most liberal term in defining the relationship between queens, even if they're not from the same drag family. "She's my sister, but I can't stand her."

DRAG QUEEN (n) — A person who uses costume and signifiers to perform and explore femininity. "She's this drag queen you have to follow on Instagram!"

ELEGANZA EXTRAVAGANZA — Having the highest amounts of elegance. "She's serving eleganza extravaganza!"

FEELING MY OATS — To appreciate oneself, to savour the beauty in the experience of being you. "Give me a moment, I'm feeling my oats!"

FOR THE GODS — Abbreviated version of "fit for the gods", describing an act performed absolutely flawlessly. "She was cinched for the gods!"

GAG (v) — To react with shock, can be good or bad depending on intonation. "Gag at those shoes Mama!"

GEISH (n) — A drag performer's wardrobe or selection of outfits. Derived from the word "Geisha". "She looked so good all in her full Geish!"

GIVING ME LIFE — A phrase of praise to demonstrate how much you love something. "Hunty, those boots are giving me life!"

HERSTORY (n) — A feminine reinterpretation of the word history. "Honey, you need to know your herstory!"

HENNY (n) — another way to say "honey", one of endearment. "You look flawless henny!"

HOUSE DOWN BOOTS — A term used to replace an exclamation mark. "She walked the house down boots!"

HUNTY (n) — A combination of the terms "Hun" and "Cunt", a term of endearment between two queens. "Hunty, you gotta share your tips!"

JUDY (n) — A dear friend. "She's a real Judy!"

KAI-KAI (v) — The act of drag queens having sex with each other. "Did you see those two heading home to kai-kai?"

KI-KI (n) — A term used for gossip, small talk, chatting, or a heart-to-heart between queens. "Let's have a ki-ki?"

LIBRARY (n) — The space opened by drag folk in which there's free rein to read each other. Born from the colloquialisms of *Paris is Burning*. "The library is officially open!"

MAMA/MAWMA/MOMMA (n) — A term of adoration

and respect among drag scenes, usually directed to more experienced or older queens, but not always. "Yes Mawma, slay!"

MUG (n) — A name for the face. "Girl, get out of my mirror, I'm beating my mug!"

PADDING (n) — Cushions made from foam or sponge strapped to the hips, the legs and the breasts to create the illusion of a different figure. "She's padded for the Gods!"

PAINTED (n) — When a queen applies a lot of makeup to achieve a certain look, usually beautifully. "Damn, she is painted like a goddess!"

PURSE FIRST — To enter a room putting one's purse first. Popularised by Bob the Drag Queen. "Walk into the room purse first!"

READ (v) — To cleverly expose someone's flaws, hence reading them like a book. Originating from the vernacular of *Paris is Burning*. "She read you for filth!"

REALNESS (n) — To appear convincing or authentic, relating often to specific categories — femme realness, butch realness, executive realness. Originating from the vernacular of *Paris is Burning*. "Honey you're serving construction worker realness!"

SERVE (v) — To offer something specific, and to offer it well. "You're serving Madonna Blonde Ambition realness!"

SHADE (n) — A form of insult. Unlike reading, shade is a more blunt demonstration of a person's flaws. "She threw you some serious shade!"

SICK'NING (adj) — To be iconic, amazing, excessively brilliant. "Girl that was sick'ning!"

SLAY (v) — To be on point or outstanding. "Honey, you slayed the dancefloor!"

T/TEE/TEA (n) — Gossip, news or information, often thought to be the truth. "What. Is. The. Tea?"

TUCK (v/n) — When a drag performer pulls back their genitals to create the appearance of a flat crotch. Duct tape, tights or tucking panties are often used to keep everything in position. "Hang on a sec queen, I'm just tucking!"

MEATY TUCK (n) — A lumpy or bulging tuck, poorly executed. "She was packing a meaty tuck tonight!"

WERK (v) — To give an outstanding presentation. "You better werk!"

YASSSS — A bastardisation of the word "yes", used to encourage or excite. "Yassss kiiiiing!"

What's Your Drag Name?

Your drag name is the first and last thing people remember about you. When you're announced on stage the MC will call it, when you release your drag album it will be emblazoned across the cover, when you star in your drag movie it will be the name called at the Oscars, when you start your drag family it will become your legacy. And, really, your name dictates your persona (although of course there's wriggle room). A Broadway queen, for example, might go by something softer, a boyband king might choose something cheesy, a pageant queen might be part of a pageanting dynasty like the Davenports or Taylors.

Your drag name can be anything, as long as it reflects the way you want to feel in drag. Some people like to take the name of their first pet as their forename, and their childhood street as their surname, for instance. Others like to think of a person they aspire to be like and join their "family" by taking a surname. It's up to you. But for starters, here's an A to Z name-a-queen bot. Simply take your initials and create your name. Remember — extra points for creativity, so adding a comma here, a pun in inverted commas there, or a Ms/Dr/Diva before will make you stand out from the already glittering crowd.

First Name

A: Aphrodite
B: Bette, Darling
C: Crystal
D: Divine
E: Elektra
F: Fister
G: Gia

H: Queen Honolulu
I: Ivanka
J: Justice
K: Karbohydrate
L: Lactasia
M: Mercedes

N: Nova Scotia
O: Opulent
P: Pollyanna
Q: Qwerty
R: Raquel
S: Sonique

T: Tatiana
U: Universe
V: Vavrinka
W: Wendy
X: Xena
Y: Yarra
Z: Zodiac

Second Name

A: Anderson
B: Bends
C: Calamity
D: Du Naughty
E: Eleganza
F: Fister
G: Greene

H: Hercules
I: Intravenous
J: Jambon
K: Kute
L: La Denim
M: Majesty

N: Never-Say-Never
O: O'Hara
P: Plastic
Q: The Drag Queen
R: Romanov
S: Sister

T: Testosterone
U: Uwanka
V: Volatility
W: Wonder
X: X-istential
Y: Yes Yes Yes!
Z: Zofia

What Type Of Drag Queen Are You?

1. **You've got to dress for a party, but you've only got an hour to get ready. What on earth do you do?**

a. Pack a pair of heels, pull on your most torn jean shorts, and throw on your makeup on the cab ride over. You know you look iconic in whatever you wear.

b. Cancel! An hour's no time to set the wig, bake the face, and get into full prim and proper character.

c. Turn up an hour and a half late, looking perfect, but with a rolodex full of classic references with a bitterly comic twist.

d. You don't do parties, just activist meetings.

2. **Choose an icon:**

a. David Bowie was the most radical artist to ever exist. Period.

b. Michelle Obama or Vanessa Williams. I can't decide, but they're both perfect examples of how to do good in the world.

c. Barbra! Judy! Liza!

d. Anyone who can play the guitar and fuck with the system.

3. Pick a colour:

a. Anything metallic and tight. Or ripped up, bleached out denim.

b. Pink! To make the boys wink!

c. Leopard print, black sequins or blue velvet.

d. All black everything.

4. You're on a date, and the person you're sat with seems tentative about the fact you do drag. You:

a. Take some glitter out of your purse, douse both of you in it, and show them the glorious ropes at the nearest queer basement party.

b. Act politely and properly, but give them no kiss and delete their number the moment you get home. Conflict isn't your style, but neither is queerphobia.

c. Make a brilliant joke out of it, one which undermines their outdated opinion. Then, if you're feeling it, take them home and show them how it's really done.

d. School your date on the patriarchal structures that lead to this kind of dragphobia, reminding them that all the rights we have as queers were built on the back of drag performers, trans folk and gender nonconformists.

5. Which scene are you most likely to be found working it on?

a. London. It's one big creative melting pot.

b. Anywhere in the Southern States of the USA.

c. In the smoky jazz clubs of Hollywood, sixty years ago, darling.

d. Brooklyn. It's where all the rad shit happens.

6. If you could be born in another era, what would it be?

a. The '90s. Everyone was fucking, taking and dancing to everything.

b. The '50s. Traditions are wonderful, and bucking them is even better.

c. The '20s. Flapper dresses, back-alley booze, the Golden Age of Hollywood. What could be more glorious?

d. The '80s/ancient Greece. In the '80s everyone was an activist. In ancient Greece, democracy worked.

7. Finding a new outfit is:

a.   Easy. I look good in everything and anything, it just takes a little editing.

b.   Well, it's all about the right fabric. Once I've got that I can make absolutely anything.

c.   Takes fucking forever. You try finding a top which looks like it belonged to Liza and doesn't make you look a hundred.

d.   Simple – a leather jacket, fishnets and docs.

8. Friend: I'm obsessed with the Kardashians.
You:

a.   They make me laugh, but they're too obsessed with their looks.

b.   They're classless. How they've become our icons I'll never know.

c.   I'm obsessed. They're so trashy but so glam at the same time. Just like me.

d.   Literally fuck fame. Literally fuck capitalism.

9. Gay rights, where are we?

a.   I'm not necessarily concerned with gay rights. I'm more into aliens.

b.   I think it's fabulous that we can, finally, marry! Now just to find a man…

c.   The best thing about gay marriage is gay divorce, honey!

d.   We've assimilated and abandoned our radical queer forbears.

10. What does drag mean to you?

a.   A chance to fuck with it all, and to fuck with my parents.

b.   A chance to put more beauty, light and grace into a dark world!

c.   It's the perfect costume to go with my savage sense of humour.

d.   It's a vessel for my radical politics.

Mostly A's: Gender Fuck

Also known as the Anti-Queen, Gender Fucks do exactly that: fuck with gender. Combining signifiers of masculine and feminine, the whole basis of this kind of drag is found in blurring gender codes, not leaning into them. Your goal is to agitate, to provoke and to push new boundaries. We can find you at clubs, in bars, on doors and tearing it up on stage.

Mostly B's: The Pageant Queen

Pageant Queens mean business. It's absolutely all about polish, perfection and professionalism. Drag, for these queens, is about female impersonation so you'll likely love to pad, paint your nails and lacquer your wigs within an inch of their life. You love to compete, yes, but you prefer to win. You can be found delivering flawless lip-syncs and beautifully put together answers á la Miss America anywhere on the pageant circuit.

Mostly C's: Campy and Catty

Humour is your gig, and camp culture is your reference bank. You're all about exaggeration, satire and indecency. Camp isn't just a style, however, it's a lifestyle: your humour spilling over into your everyday life. You can be found stealing the spotlight in comedy clubs, or watching *The Wizard of Oz*, once again, while practising your makeup.

Mostly D's: The Activist

The backbone of drag is the politics that come with it. While some queens and kings believe that drag is political in and of itself, which is true, you actively pursue the political history and present of what drag really means. You can be found in a leather jacket lip-synching to Siouxsie and the Banshees, when you're not at an activist organising meeting, that is.

Acknowledgements

All my love goes to my community — the LGBTQIA+ community — who have taught both me, and so much of the world, how to live brilliantly. Specific mentions go to the trans and non-binary folk and people of colour who are so often left out of LGBTQIA+ narratives and history, who are the most important within it. More love to my queer family, my glorious sisters in Denim, and my queen Hatty Carman. Special mention goes to the iconic and wonderful Zoe Ross, who is the master in making dreams come true.

Crystal
x